# LEARN JAVASCRIPT IN 1 HOUR

# Learn JavaScript in 1 Hour

by John Bura

Copyright © 2016 Mammoth Interactive, Inc. All rights reserved.

Printed in Canada.

Published by Mammoth Interactive, Inc., 218 – 111 West Broadway, Vancouver, British Columbia, Canada
V5Y 1P4.

Mammoth Interactive books may be purchased for educational, business, or sales promotional use.

**Writer:** John Bura
**Transcriber:** Chelsea Cuffy
**Editor:** Alexandra Kropova

November 2016: First Edition

# ABOUT THE AUTHOR

John Bura has been programming since 1997 and teaching since 2002. John brings a unique perspective with his years of experience of teaching and real-world experience running a software company. In 2008, John founded Mammoth Interactive.

Since then, his company has sold over 400,000 copies of educational courses around the world. Their courses have been featured on websites such as Venture Beat, Expert Dojo, Cult of Mac, and Macgams. In addition, Mammoth Interactive has produced games for the iPhone, iPad, XBOX 360, and more. The organization also has a long history of providing support to other developers. Mammoth Interactive has been contracted to produce epic soundtracks, addicting levels, rock solid programming, and business development.

Go to **www.mammothinteractive.com** to get free stuff, courses, books, apps, games, t-shirts, daily deals, and more!

# www.mammothinteractive.com

# TABLE OF CONTENTS

**Introduction** ........................................................................................................5
HTML .....................................................................................................................5
CSS......................................................................................................................... 6
JavaScript ..............................................................................................................7
**CHAPTER 1:** Adding Functions ...................................................................... 8
Scaling Functions ................................................................................................10
**CHAPTER 2:** Changing Text in JavaScript ..................................................... 12
**CHAPTER 3:** Variables ..................................................................................... 14
**CHAPTER 4:** Arrays .........................................................................................18
**CHAPTER 5:** Objects ....................................................................................... 21
**CHAPTER 6:** Variable Scope .......................................................................... 24
**CHAPTER 7:** Adding User Input Text ............................................................27
**CHAPTER 8:** Calling Functions...................................................................... 29
**CHAPTER 9:** If Statements............................................................................. 31
Else If and Else Statements ............................................................................... 34
**CHAPTER 10:** Changing the Style with JavaScript ....................................... 39
Conclusion and Challenge ................................................................................ 43

# INTRODUCTION

JavaScript provides the foundation for web design. If you are unfamiliar with HTML, check out our eBook "Learning How to Code in HTML". If you already have a bit of a foundation, then we will work with that.

To follow along with our examples, go to jsbin.com, which can run on a Mac, PC, or mobile device. This site is an editor that will allow you to see your creations in real time.

Three major languages make up the internet: HTML, CSS, and JavaScript. HTML stands for Hypertext Markup Language. Being a markup language, HTML is not used to make calculations. Instead, it gives a basic foundation. CSS stands for Cascading Style Sheets, which is used to design a website. We set everything up in HTML. We use CSS to make modifications and set up the color, font, and background of a site. JavaScript adds functionality. JavaScript does calculations and many other functions that we have come to expect from computers.

Keeping the Output tab open in jsbin will allow you to see you progress as you edit code in real time.

# HTML

Tags in HTML are made up of triangle brackets. There are opening and closing tags. For instance, **<p>** is an opening paragraph tag. To complete the function, we must close the tag. A closing tag is simply the opening tag with a slash: **</p>**. Some tags are self-closing, which means they don't require closing tags. However, for the most part, we will always have to close the tags ourselves.

In jsbin.com, open the HTML tab, and type in the following code:

```
<!DOCTYPE html>
<html>
   <body>
      <p>Tags</p>

   </body>
 </html>
```

# CSS

CSS focuses on aesthetics. By opening the CSS tab in jsbin, we can modify our paragraph text with `p{`. Make sure you close the command with an opposite curly bracket `}`. For instance, if we want to change the color of our paragraph text to red, we can say:

```
p{
   color: red;
}
```

# JAVASCRIPT

JavaScript adds functionality to a website. To code in JavaScript, type in a command, and end each command with a semi-colon. The semi-colon tells the compiler, which runs code, that the line is done. The console is used to add and look at specific JavaScript code. For instance, type in **alert ("Tags");**.

```
alert("Tags");
```

The quote within the alert command means that the compiler will print a string. The string is our character. The Output page will allow us to see our function when we click "Run with JS".

# CHAPTER 1: ADDING FUNCTIONS

Why don't we put the alert we created to good use? We can have a JavaScript course that is very practical without HTML. Let's hop into the HTML tag and create a button. In order to do that, we must add in a button tag **&lt;button&gt;**. Within that tag, we will command an onclick function named **myAwesomeFunction**: **&lt;button onclick= "myAwesomeFunction()"&gt;**.

 It is important to include the parentheses after the function name.

After the sharp bracket **&gt;**, you can choose the text that will be displayed on the button. After that, don't forget to close the button tag with **&lt;/button&gt;**.

```
<!DOCTYPE html>
<html>

<body>
 <p>Tags</p>

   <button onclick= "myAwesomeFunction()"> Function</button>
</body>
</html>
```

Close the HTML tab, and open the JavaScript tab instead. Delete the alert tab, and enter the function we just input into HTML.

```
function myAwesomeFunction(){
}
```

So we just created a function. But what is a function, anyway? In JavaScript, it is a place to put your code. When creating a website or web app, there are several different functions to consider such as checking the Internet connection and doing calculations. We separate our code and our function of what we do into different functions.

When declaring a function, you can follow these steps:

- Type in the word function: **function**
- Type in the name of the function: **function myAwesomeFunction**
- Add two round brackets: **function myAwesomeFunction()**
- In curly brackets after that, enter your alert: **function myAwesomeFunction(){alert("Function")}**

Back in the HTML tab, remember we had that onclick? That onclick says when we click, it will call **myAwesomeFunction**. Everything in the same line as the function in JavaScript is going to be run. In this case, because we entered an alert command, that command will run.

> Place a semi-colon at the end of each command that is in between the curly brackets. Do not place them at the end of the curly brackets.

```
function myAwesomeFunction(){
    alert("Function");
}
```

To verify that the code works, click the "Run with JS" button in the Output tab.

> Functions are case-sensitive. If you type a function in uppercase in the HTML tab, it must be uppercase in the JavaScript tab. Copying and pasting the function from HTML to JavaScript will help you make sure they match.

# SCALING FUNCTIONS

When designing a website or app, you'll most probably have multiple functions. Therefore, you will often have to scale functions.

To scale a function, open the HTML tab, and modify the **onclick** command so that it says **&lt;button onclick= "functionOne()"&gt; 1 &lt;/button&gt;**. Then copy and paste that line 3 times. Label the functions 1 through 4.

```
<!DOCTYPE html>
<html>

<body>
 <p>Tags</p>

   <button onclick= "functionOne()">1</button>
   <button onclick= "functionTwo()">2</button>
   <button onclick= "functionThree()">3</button>
   <button onclick= "functionFour()">4</button>
</body>
</html>
```

Next we need to open the JavaScript tab and transcribe the functions in HTML over to JavaScript.

```
function functionOne(){
    alert("1");
}
```

If you select the Output tab and click "Run with JS", you will see the script run. If a pop-up shows up when you click the box labeled 1, then the script was successful. If nothing happens, check that the function was written in HTML the same way as it was in JavaScript.

Now we will finish this function with the other buttons.

```
function functionOne(){
    alert("1");
}
function functionTwo(){
    alert("2");
}
function functionThree(){
    alert("3");
}
function functionFour(){
    alert("4");
}
```

Often when you code a web application, you end up using a lot of functions. A simple app could have 10 or even 50 functions! For every thing that your app does, you will want to write a new function. If the app needs to update, that's a function. If it needs to print, that's a function. If it needs to calculate, that's another function. If you, for instance, need to calculate three different things at three different times, your code will contain three separate functions.

There are two reasons for doing this: to make your game work and look better.

# CHAPTER 2: CHANGING TEXT IN JAVASCRIPT

For the purpose of our next example, let's clear our JavaScript code and delete all of our buttons in HTML except for one. Next we will name our function **changeTheText** because we will in fact be changing the text.

```
<!DOCTYPE html>
<html>

<body>
 <p>Tags</p>

   <button onclick= "changeTheText()"> Change The Text</button>
</body>
</html>
```

Open the JavaScript page, and add in the **changeTheText** function.

```
function changeTheText(){

}
```

We will be modifying our paragraph tag. Go back to the HTML tag, and give the paragraph tag an ID by writing **<p id = "paragraphText">Tags</p>**.

> Each specific tag that we want to change gets an ID, and there is only one ID per tag.

```
<!DOCTYPE html>
<html>

<body>
 <p id= "paragraphText">Tags</p>

   <button onclick= "changeTheText()"> Change The Text</button>
</body>
</html>
```

Right now, this paragraph tag has the ID **paragraphtext**. Hence, we can reference this in JavaScript and change the tag like so:

```
function changeTheText(){
document.getElementById('paragraphText').innerHTML =
"AWESOME!";
}
```

Run the code in the Output tab. The text should have changed to what you had the function equal.

Let's break down what just happened. We have a button that calls the function **changeTheText**. This function will change the text. If we put **document.getElementById('paragraphText')** outside the function, it will just automatically call the function.

But what if we only want to call this function at a specific time? The command **getElementById** (whose casing is important) gets the tag we input into HTML by the ID. Therefore, if we use a different ID, the function will not work. The **.innerHTML** of this tag changes to "**AWESOME!**"

# CHAPTER 3: VARIABLES

Variables are crucial to programming regardless of the language you're using. A variable is like a box into which you can put one piece of data, such as a number of character.

 You cannot put both numbers and characters into one box.

To declare a variable, first visit the JavaScript tab. Write in the number you would like to declare using the keyword var. In this example, we'll declare a variable named **variableNumber**. In computer programming, this is known as a **declaration**. Giving the variable a value, such as **23**, is known as **initialization**. Do not forget to add a semi-colon to the end of the line.

```
var variableNumber = 23;

function changeTheText(){
document.getElementById('paragraphText').innerHTML =
"AWESOME!";
}
```

**variableNumber** will always equal **23**. If we make `.innerHTML` equal to **variableNumber**, the Output will change to **23**.

```
var variableNumber = 23;

function changeTheText(){
document.getElementById('paragraphText').innerHTML =
variableNumber;
}
```

Open the Output tab and click "Run with JS". Then click the button "Change The

Text". As you can see, the text changes to "23" because we made the `innerHTML` equal to our `variableNumber`, which was 23. It will change to which ever number you decide to make the variable number equal.

In JavaScript, we can mash variable numbers accordingly. On the other hand, in other programming languages, numbers are categorized into floats and integers. **Floats** refer to numbers containing decimals. **Integers** are only positive or negative whole numbers.

```
var variableNumber= 55;
var float = 34.5;
var int = 23;
```

In JavaScript, we can mix floats and integers, whereas in other languages we couldn't.

Let's take a look at another variable type: the **string**. The string variable is full of characters rather than numbers. Use the same keyword `var` to create `variableString`, and give it the value `Awesome!`.

> The value of a string variable must be in quotation marks.

Also, make `innerHTML` equal to this new variable.

```
var variableNumber = 55;
var variableString= "Awesome!";

function changeTheText(){
document.getElementById('paragraphText').innerHTML = variableString;
}
```

Open the Output tab, click "Run with JS", and click our "Change The Text" button. The text should become "Awesome!"

Now watch what happens when we integrate the number variable with the string variable by typing:

```
var variableNumber = 55;
var variableString= "Awesome!";

function changeTheText(){
document.getElementById('paragraphText').innerHTML =
variableString; + variableNumber;
}
```

Open the Output tab, click Run with JS, then click our Change The Text button. The text should now read both your string and number variable "Awesome!55".

Notice how there is no space between the exclamation point and 55? For there to be a space, add a space at the end of the exclamation point in our string variable.

```
var variableNumber = 55;
var variableString= "Awesome! ";

function changeTheText(){
document.getElementById('paragraphText').innerHTML =
variableString; + variableNumber;
}
```

If we enter **variableNumber= variableNumber + 10** into our **changeTheText** function; watch what happens to our text.

```
var variableNumber = 55;
var variableString= "Awesome! ";

function changeTheText(){
   variableNumber = variableNumber + 10;

document.getElementById('paragraphText').innerHTML =
variableString; + variableNumber;
}
```

Open the Output tab, click "Run with JS", then click our "Change The Text" button. You will notice the function add 10 to our original variable number!

# CHAPTER 4: ARRAYS

When we talk about computer programming and web development, we talk about how data is handled. In the previous chapter, we discussed how variables are like boxes into which we can place a piece of data. However, what happens when we have multiple pieces of data? In this case, we can use arrays. If a variable is like a box, and array is like an egg carton.

To create a sample array, use the following format. Let's have our array contain items 0 through 4.

```
var variableNumber = 33;
var variableString = "Awesome! ";

var numberArray = [0,1,2,3,4];

function changeTheText(){
  variableNumber = variableNumber + 10 ;


document.getElementById('paragraphText').innerHTML = variableString; + variableNumber;
}
```

Furthermore, we should make the `innerHTML` equal `numberArray[]`.

> The numbers of which a number array is made up are enclosed in square brackets. Likewise, `innerHTML` must end in square brackets (before the semi-colon, of course).

```
var variableNumber = 33;
var variableString = "Awesome! ";

var numberArray = [0,1,2,3,4];

function changeTheText(){
   variableNumber = variableNumber + 10 ;

document.getElementById('paragraphText').innerHTML = numberArray[];
}
```

The compiler will print numbers 0 through 4.

Square brackets are an indicator that an array is present. This is universal across most programming languages. Whenever you see square brackets, you can safely assume that they correspond to an array.

See what happens when you type in a number such as **0** into the square brackets of the number array in `innerHTML`. By running the code and clicking our button, you will see the text change to the number we put in the array.

Arrays have **indexes**. Indexes are the numbers we plugged into our number array variable: `var numberArray = [0,1,2,3,4];`. Here we have the zero index, the one index, the two index, the three index, and the four index.

If we change those numbers to **5,6,1,9,8**; **5** would still be considered index zero, **6** would be index one, **9** would be index two, **1** would be index three, and **8** would be index four.

Let's test this theory. Input another index, such as 3, in the number array's brackets in innerHTML: `.innerHTML = numberArray[3]`.

In the Output tab, select "Run with JS", and click on our button. The Output will change to the number 9.

Now try accessing an index that is out of range by typing in a number greater than 4 in the square brackets: `.innerHTML = numberArray[5]`.

If we run this function in the Output tab, we will get a message that reads "undefined".

Some programming languages crash the program if we try to access an array that is out of its range. Luckily, accessing an array out of range in JavaScript does not crash the program. Regardless, it's advised not to try to do so too often.

Most programming languages will not allow us to mix number variables and characters in one array. Although JavaScript permits mixing, it is still in best practice to separate number variables and string variables (characters) on two separate lines.

If we change our code to match the following, the compiler will print "C".

```
var variableNumber = 33;
var variableString = "Awesome! ";

var numberArray = [0,1,2,3,4];
var stringArray = ["A", "B", "C"];

function changeTheText(){
   variableNumber = variableNumber + 10 ;


document.getElementById('paragraphText').innerHTML = stringArray[2];
}
```

# CHAPTER 5: OBJECTS

Imagine you have an apple in front of you. That apple has weight, volume, color, and taste. Similarly, objects as data types have different properties. When it comes to computer programming, we must take objects and input them into computers.

Let's make a new variable using an object. In this example, that will be a car. More specifically, it will be a red Tesla with a range of 475 *kilometers (km)* and a sunroof, and whose top speed is 250 kilometers per hour.

```
var variableNumber = 33;
var variableString = "Awesome! ";

var numberArray = [0,1,2,3,4];
var stringArray = ["A", "B", "C"];

var car ={name: "Tesla", range: 475, unit: "km", color: "Red",
topSpeed: 250, sunRoof:"Yes"};

function changeTheText(){
   variableNumber = variableNumber + 10 ;
```

The range and top speed properties are not in quotations because quotations are used for characters and do not enable us to do mathematical calculations.

Let's make the `innerHTML` equal the properties name and range: `.innerHTML = car.name + car.range;`.

```
var variableNumber = 33;
var variableString = "Awesome! ";

var numberArray = [0,1,2,3,4];
var stringArray = ["A", "B", "C"];

var car ={name: "Tesla", range: 475, unit: "km", color: "Red",
topSpeed: 250, sunRoof:"Yes"};

function changeTheText(){
   variableNumber = variableNumber + 10 ;


document.getElementById('paragraphText').innerHTML = car.name
+ car.range;
}
```

By running the code, you should see "Tesla475" on your screen. Notice that there is no space in between the two properties? To correct this, we can create a space variable.

```
var variableNumber = 33;
var variableString = "Awesome! ";

var space = " ";

var numberArray = [0,1,2,3,4];
var stringArray = ["A", "B", "C"];

var car ={name: "Tesla", range: 475, unit: "km", color: "Red",
topSpeed: 250, sunRoof:"Yes"};

function changeTheText(){
   variableNumber = variableNumber + 10 ;


document.getElementById('paragraphText').innerHTML = car.name
+ space + car.range;
}
```

Run the JavaScript in the Output tab. There will now be a space between the words "Tesla" and "475". Let's continue adding the rest of our car's properties while including spaces.

```
var variableNumber = 33;
var variableString = "Awesome!" ;

var space = " ";

var numberArray = [0,1,2,3,4];
var stringArray = [ "A", "B", "C"];
var car ={name: "Tesla", range: 475, unit: "km", color: "Red",
topSpeed: 250, sunRoof:"Yes"};

function changeTheText(){
   variableNumber = variableNumber + 10 ;

document.getElementById('paragraphText').innerHTML = car.name +
space + car.range +  car.unit + space + car.color + space +
car.topSpeed + car.unit + space + car.sunRoof;
}
```

Go ahead and run the function on the Output tab. Your screen should say "Tesla 475km Red 250km Yes".

> Remember that variables are case-sensitive. When inputting variables into functions, be sure the spelling and capitalization are correct. Otherwise the function will not work.

# CHAPTER 6: VARIABLE SCOPE

Before moving on, clear your JavaScript page so that you are left with the following:

```
var variableNumber = 33;

function changeTheText(){
document.getElementByID ('paragraphText').innerHTML = 5;
}
```

When we declare a variable at the top of the page, we can use that variable throughout that entire page.

If we add another function called **printScore**, we can use another variable number with that function and set it to any number we want.

```
var variableNumber = 33;

function changeTheText(){
document.getElementByID ('paragraphText').innerHTML = 5;
}

function printScore(){
  variableNumber = 23;
```

We can use variable numbers with multiple functions. It does not matter if we have one function, ten functions, twenty functions, etc. We can use variable numbers in each one of those functions. However, if we declare a variable within the curly brackets, we can only use the variable within those curly brackets.

Let's make a scope variable.

```
var variableNumber = 33;

function changeTheText(){
  var scopeVariable = 11;

document.getElementByID ('paragraphText').innerHTML =
scopeVariable;
}

function printScore(){
   scopeVariable = 23;
```

Notice how, in our first function, two scope variables turned blue? That means the computer is recognizing this function. Try adding our scope variable to our second function.

```
var variableNumber = 33;

function changeTheText(){
  var scopeVariable = 11;

document.getElementByID ('paragraphText').innerHTML =
scopeVariable;
}

function printScore(){
  scopeVariable = 33;
}
```

Notice how the scope variable in our second function did not change colors? The computer is not able to read the second function because our scope variable cannot reach beyond its scope. The scope of our scope variable is in between the curly brackets.

```
var variableNumber = 33;

function changeTheText(){
  var scopeVariable = 11;

document.getElementByID ('paragraphText').innerHTML = scopeVariable;
}

function printScore(){
  scopeVariable = 33;
}
```

We can declare multiple scope variables as long as they are in separate curly brackets.

```
var variableNumber = 33;

function changeTheText(){
  var scopeVariable = 11;

document.getElementByID ('paragraphText').innerHTML = scopeVariable;
}

function printScore(){
  var scopeVariable = 55;
  scopeVariable = 33;
}
```

# CHAPTER 7: ADDING USER INPUT TEXT

To add user inputs, we must add in an input tag into our HTML. There are many different type of inputs. The one that we are concerned with right now is the text input. We will attach an ID to this input as well. Note that this input tag does not need a closing tag.

```
<!DOCTYPE html>
<html>

<body>
 <p id= "paragraphText">Tags</p>
 <input type = 'text' id = 'changeUserText'>

   <button onclick= "changeTheText()"> Change The Text</button>
</body>
</html>
```

Hop back into the JavaScript tab, and delete the scope variables. Next we will insert our input variable within the scope of this function.

```
Function changeTheText(){
    var userInputText

document.getElementById('paragraphText').innerHTML = scopeVariable;
```

Notice that when we declare a variable, the first word is all lowercase, and the following words begin with an uppercase letter: **userInputText**. This is called **camel casing**. It is used to make code look more organized.

Let's add our input from HTML into our JavaScript. It must be written in the exact same way as the ID in HTML. To ensure that the spelling and casing are identical, you can copy and paste the ID from HTML into JavaScript.

```
Function changeTheText(){
   var userInputText
document.getElementById('changeUserText').value;

document.getElementById('paragraphText').innerHTML =
scopeVariable;
```

Open the Output tab, and run this function. Nothing will happen because we haven't actually told the function to do anything yet. Therefore, make the innerHTML equal to userInputText:

```
Function changeTheText(){
   var userInputText
document.getElementById('changeUserText').value;

document.getElementById('paragraphText').innerHTML =
userInputText;
```

Now we can run the JavaScript in the Output tab. The text you type in the box will appear in print after you press the "Change The Text" button.

To summarize user input text, first of all we can add in user inputs. As well, we can store those user inputs in a variable. This happens all the time. In fact, when you receive user data, you should store it in a variable because then you can perform necessary computing functions, such as adding.

# CHAPTER 8: CALLING FUNCTIONS

We've looked at calling the HTML and calling a specific ID to call a specific function, but we can actually call functions within JavaScript, too. To example this, let's create another function.

```
Function onClickedButton{
}

Function changeTheText(){
   var userInputText
document.getElementById('changeUserText').value;

document.getElementById('paragraphText').innerHTML = userInputText;
```

We can give this button an ID in HTML. The IDs of buttons usually begin with the prefix of the type being used. In this case, we are using a **btn** (button). We will call the onclick button "**onClickedButton**".

```
<!DOCTYPE html>
<html>

<body>
 <p id= "paragraphText">Tags</p>
 <input type = 'text' id = 'changeUserText'>
 <button id = "btnChangeTextButton" onclick = 'onClickedButton()'>Change The Text </button>

   <button onclick= "work()"> Change The Text</button>
</body>
</html>
```

29 | Learn JavaScript in 1 Hour

Right now, if we try to run the JavaScript in our Output tab, nothing will happen. We have to call upon the **changeTheText** function to our **onClickedButton** function for this to work. Oftentimes, we must call one function upon another function.

```
Function onClickedButton{
    changeTheText();
}

Function changeTheText(){
    var userInputText
document.getElementById( 'changeUserText').value;

document.getElementById('paragraphText').innerHTML =
userInputText;
```

Open the Output tab. Now if we type a message in the box and run the JavaScript, our message will come out in print once we click "Change The Text".

Remember that a computer reads code line by line. The compiler reads the function **onClickButton**, and this code only gets run when we click "Change The Text". When we click the button, it tells the computer to run another function.

# CHAPTER 9: IF STATEMENTS

If statements are important even if you are an advanced coder because we end up running if statements in almost every program. If statements also occur in real-life situations: if it is raining outside, wear a rain jacket. If you are hungry, go eat. These examples have a condition and an action to them. That is the basic idea behind if statements in code.

Let's create an if statement. Clear the JavaScript tab. We are going to add a number variable equal to 12.

```
var someNumber = 12;

var changeVariable = 0;

if(someNumber == 12){
   changeVariable = 1;
}

document.getElementById ('paragraphText').innerHTML = changeVariable;
```

This if statement states that if **someNumber** equals **12**, then the compiler will run the line **changeVariable= 1**. If **someNumber** does not equal **12**, then the compiler will skip the line **changeVariable**.

Open the Output tab, and run the JavaScript. "1" will appear on your screen.

There are a couple other equations that we can try. For instance, we can have the compiler print "1" if **someNumber** is less than 13. In this case, the condition would be true because our variable is 12.

```
var someNumber = 12;

var changeVariable = 0;

if(someNumber < 13){
   changeVariable = 1;
}

document.getElementById ('paragraphText').innerHTML = changeVariable;
```

Run the JavaScript. The compiler will print **changeVariable**, which is 1, proving our statement true.

What if we want the compiler to print **changeVariable** only if **someNumber** is less than 12? To try this, change the **13** in our if statement to **12**.

```
var someNumber = 12;

var changeVariable = 0;

if(someNumber < 12){
   changeVariable = 1;
}

document.getElementById ('paragraphText').innerHTML = changeVariable;
```

If you run this function, "0" will appear on your screen because the statement is false. Since **someNumber** is not less than 12, the computer skipped the **changeVariable** line in our code.

For our next example, let's see what happens to our code when it looks like this:

```
var someNumber = 12;

var changeVariable = 0;

if(someNumber ! 13){
   changeVariable = 1;
}

document.getElementById ('paragraphText').innerHTML = changeVariable;
```

This if statement says that if **someNumber** does NOT equal 13, **changeVariable** will equal 1.

If statements are important because sometimes, when running a program, we have to account for an action that, although may not happen often, can crash our code.

# ELSE IF AND ELSE STATEMENTS

This section covers else if statements. Begin by creating one such statement:

```
var someNumber = 12;

var changeVariable = 0;

if(someNumber ! 13){
   changeVariable = 1;
}

else if (someNumber == 12){
   changeVariable = 2;
}

document.getElementById ('paragraphText').innerHTML = changeVariable;
```

By running the JavaScript on this function, you will notice that our else if statement gets skipped because our if statement is true.

Make `someNumber` in the if statement equal to 13.

```
var someNumber = 12;

var changeVariable = 0;

if(someNumber == 13){
   changeVariable = 1;
}

else if (someNumber == 12){
   changeVariable = 2;
}

document.getElementById ('paragraphText').innerHTML =
changeVariable;
```

With this code, the else if statement will be called because when the if statement is proven false, the compiler goes to the else if statement.

Let's add another else if statement. Note: do not make the other else if statements the same as the first one. That is considered bad programming because it is redundant.

```
var someNumber = 12;

var changeVariable = 0;

if(someNumber == 13){
   changeVariable = 1;
}

else if (someNumber == 12){
   changeVariable = 2;
}

else if (someNumber == 11){
  changeVariable = 3;
}

document.getElementById ('paragraphText').innerHTML = changeVariable;
```

Additionally, if we make the variable **someNumber** equal **11**, the compiler will call our second else if statement.

```
var someNumber = 11;

var changeVariable = 0;

if(someNumber == 13){
   changeVariable = 1;
}

else if (someNumber == 12){
   changeVariable = 2;
}

else if (someNumber == 11){
  changeVariable = 3;
}

document.getElementById ('paragraphText').innerHTML = changeVariable;
```

Run the JavaScript in the Output tab, and a "3" will show up on the screen because our second else if statement is true and our other else if and if statements are false.

There is another item we can add in: an **else statement**. To demonstrate this, let's make `someNumber` equal `10` and add in an else statement.

```
var someNumber = 10;

var changeVariable = 0;

if(someNumber == 13){
   changeVariable = 1;
}

else if (someNumber == 12){
   changeVariable = 2;
}

else if (someNumber == 11){
  changeVariable = 3;
}

else{
   changeVariable = 4;
}

document.getElementById ('paragraphText').innerHTML = changeVariable;
```

The compiler will print "4" because all the other statements are false. An else statement will only run if all the other if and else if statements are incorrect.

You may be thinking: When do we use all these statements? The best practice is: If you need an if statement, write an if statement. Else if statements help categorize something even more specifically.

Furthermore, you generally do not want to have an else statement as the main logic. For the most part, else statements are reserved for random occurrences that may or may not happen. For example, in games often a variable gets assigned a strange level that could break the game. In that instance, we could use an else statement to prevent our code from crashing.

# CHAPTER 10: CHANGING THE STYLE WITH JAVASCRIPT

Did you know that you can change the print style in JavaScript? To try this out, first delete everything in CSS, create a new slate in HTML, and create a new slate in JavaScript. Now we can add a button functionality in HTML.

```
<!DOCTYPE html>
<html>

<body>
 <p id = "paragraphText"> Tags </p>

 <button onClick = "buttonFunction()"> Click Me</button>
</body>
</html>
```

Hop back over into the JavaScript tab, and code a new function called **buttonFunction** that contains the document **getElementById**.

```
Function buttonFunction(){

   document.getElementById ('paragraphText').innerHTML = changeVariable;
}
```

To double-check if this function is working, run **innerHTML**, and run the JavaScript in the Output tab. "1" should show up on your display.

Instead of using **innerHTML = changeVariable**, we can try changing that code to **style**.

```
Function buttonFunction(){
    document.getElementById('paragraphText').style;
}
```

Before, we had the document of the entire project (**getElementById**), we picked a specific ID that we changed. Then, we set up paragraph text in HTML. Now, we also have style, which refers to style points of our document, such as color. For instance, if we make the style color orange, the color of our text will become orange.

```
Function buttonFunction(){
    document.getElementById('paragraphText').style.color = "orange";
}
```

We can change the size in megapixels, the color, and the font all on their own separate lines.

```
function buttonFunction(){
    document.getElementById('paragraphText').style.color = "orange";
    document.getElementById('paragraphText').style.fontsize = "50px";
    document.getElementById('paragraphText').style.fontfamily = "Impact";
}
```

Let's design some more buttons. To do so, open the HTML tab, and copy and paste the button function. Our first button will be **buttonFunction0**, and our second button will be **buttonFunction1**. Whenever you have multiple functions, it is beneficial to number them. We started counting at 0 because that is the number at which computers start counts. This is known as **zero base counting**. In this example, **buttonFunction0** will say "Click Me", and **buttonFunction1** will say "Another Style".

```
<!DOCTYPE html>
<html>

<body>
 <p id = "paragraphText"> Tags </p>

 <button onClick = "buttonFunction0()"> Click Me</button>

 <button onClick = "buttonFunction1()"> Another Style</button>

</body>
</html>
```

Next, open the JavaScript tab, and copy and paste the first button function. Change the properties in the second function.

```
function buttonFunction(){
 document.getElementById('paragraphText').style.color = "orange";
 document.getElementById('paragraphText').style.fontsize = "50px";
 document.getElementById('paragraphText').style.fontfamily = "Impact";
}

document.getElementById('paragraphText').style.color = "blue";
document.getElementById('paragraphText').style.fontsize = "70px";
document.getElementById('paragraphText').style.fontfamily = "Courier";
```

Open the Output tab, and run the JavaScript. As you can see, we created two separate buttons, both having different properties.

# CONCLUSION AND CHALLENGE

Congratulations! You now have a solid foundation of JavaScript knowledge. You know how to add, among other things, variables, functions, and statements. Furthermore, you are able to manipulate the style of your webpage in order to make your site stand out.

The best developers spend a lot of time experimenting with their development environment and trying out new things. So, along these lines, I'm going to give you a challenge: use what you've learned from this tutorial to create another website that acts as your portfolio. Good luck!

www.ingramcontent.com/pod-product-compliance
Lightning Source LLC
Chambersburg PA
CBHW080851170526
45158CB00009B/2709